M000012178

Presented to

_____

_____

from

A Grandmother
is someone
to celebrate!

# I Celebrate You, Grandmother!

Illustrated by Joy Marie   Written by T.J. Mills

COUNTRYMAN

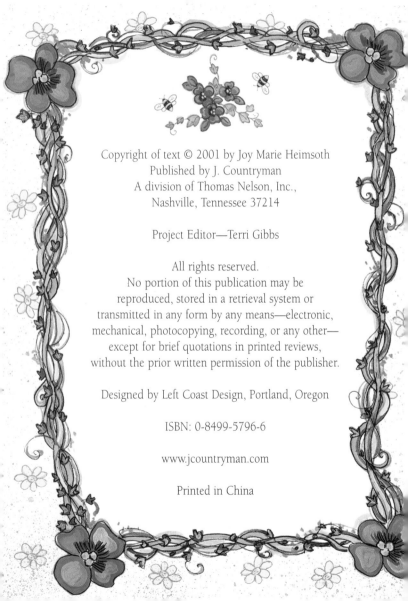

You've told me stories
that made me smile,
lived your life with
grace and style,
for the love you've
given me all the while~

Grandmother, I celebrate you!

Lavender

Devotion

I celebrate your Devotion

Grandmas are a gift
from heaven above,
with strength and devotion
that comes from God's love.

Grandmas are special
in so many ways,
their gift of comfort
will last all our days.

Looking back on all our days
Like sweet wildflowers
in a simple bouquet,
hollow accomplishments over
time will
surrender,
while sweet
simple
pleasures
are what
we'll
remember.

My sweet memory
of a special time with you:

_____

_____

_____

_____

_____

_____

_____

_____

_____

I celebrate your Patience

Chamomile
Patience

Grandma's steps
like mine are slow,
we take our time
wherever we go,
to watch or touch
or stop and see
what others pass
so hastily.

I celebrate your Faith

Verbena
Faithful

This is how you have
strengthened my faith:

_____

_____

_____

_____

_____

_____

_____

_____

A Grandmother
holds your hand
for awhile,
your spirit while she can,
and your heart
forever.

I celebrate your Kindness

Grandmother,
you bring happiness
to others by:

_____

_____

_____

_____

_____

_____

_____

_____

Sow seeds of kindness,
Gather blossoms of joy.

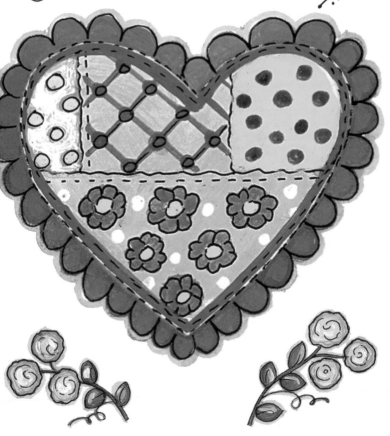

Your life is a story.
Don't leave out
the good parts.

# I celebrate your Goodness

These are some of the things I admire most about you:

_____

_____

_____

_____

_____

_____

_____

You taught me to care
you taught me to share,
but the best things
you taught me~
you taught me
through prayer.

# This is my prayer for you Grandmother

_____

_____

_____

_____

_____

_____

_____

For all the tears
you've seen me through,
All the joy and laughter too.
For all the love I hold for you,
And all the dreams
you made come true—
Grandma,
I celebrate you!